AF480729

ETERNAL
FIRST
GLANCE

ETERNAL
FIRST
GLANCE

A Sonnet Sequence
of Faithful Love

BY JOHN DAVID SMITH

Scribe and Canvas Publishing
South Carolina

Hardcover ISBN: 979-8-950061-10-3
Library of Congress Control Number: 2026941452

Published by Scribe & Canvas Publishing™
Pendleton, SC | www.scribeandcanvas.com

Interior and cover design by Elev8d Designs
Printed in the United States of America

10 9 8 7 6 5 4 3 2 1

To those who have known
the power of a single glance—
not just the moment it begins,
but the life it becomes.
To the ones who have loved,
lost,
stayed,
and still carry something of it forward.
May these poems meet you
where memory and meaning
learn to live together.

The Poet's Prelude

Eternal First Glance is not simply about the moment love begins.

It is about what that moment becomes—
over time, through change, and in the face of what it cannot keep.

These poems were first shaped by the wonder of recognition—
that quiet instant when something in us awakens to the presence of another.

But as the pages unfolded,
so did the truth.

Love did not remain untouched.

It did not stay as it first appeared.

It grew, deepened, strained,
and in some places—broke.

And still...
something remained.

This collection moves in five movements:
the glance,
the staying,

the deepening,
the breaking,
and the faithful.

Not as separate experiences,
but as one continuous unfolding—
the way love is actually lived.

These sonnets are not meant to preserve a moment.

They are meant to witness what happens
after the moment has passed.

So I invite you—
not to rush through these pages,
but to sit with them.

Let them meet your own memories,
your own questions,
your own understanding of what love has been,
and what it has left behind.

You may not find the love you first believed in.

But you may find something truer—
something that stayed,
even after everything changed.

— John David Smith

Table of Contents

I
The Glance

———— ◆ ————

"Not everything begins loudly—
some things arrive as recognition."

The Silent Quest

Alone I moved through corridors of thought,
Where hours echoed more than they revealed.
The days returned with little change or plot,
A quiet weight that would not quite be healed.

I watched the sky as if it might respond,
Or shift the stillness I had come to know.
But every distant light I leaned upon
Fell back to something I could not outgrow.

And then, not sudden—something in the air,
A softening I could not trace or name.
No voice, no sign—just how you stood there,
And how the moment did not feel the same.

No answer given, nothing to pursue—
Yet something in me turned... and turned to you.

A Rose of Dawn

The world had settled into muted tone,
A quiet field where nothing new would rise.
I moved through days that felt already known,
And learned to live with absence undisguised.

I did not call it loss—just something missed,
A space that stayed where something might have grown.
A place I carried gently in my chest,
Without expecting it to be outgrown.

Then morning came, not brighter than before,
But somehow holding more than it had been.
And in that light, without becoming more,
I felt a shift begin somewhere within.

No sudden bloom, no change I could foresee—
Just how your presence opened space in me.

Echoes of a Call

The nights stretched on, unmarked by anything,
A steady drift I had no need to name.
The silence held a kind of quiet ring,
Not harsh—but always, somehow, still the same.

I listened not for voices in the dark,
Nor waited for a sign to lead me through;
But something moved—so slight, it left no mark,
Except the way it seemed to draw toward you.

No words were formed, no message made complete,
No truth declared for me to understand.
Just how the moment felt less incomplete
The closer that I found myself to stand.

No call I heard, no voice I could construe—
Yet something in the silence pointed you.

Whispers in the Wind

The years had passed like weather over ground,
Leaving their mark, then fading as they went.
I learned to read the quiet in the sound
Of days that held no clear accomplishment.

The wind would move through spaces left undone,
A restless touch across what time had worn.
It carried fragments I could not outrun,
Yet never shaped them into something born.

And then it changed—not louder, not more clear,
But something in its movement felt more near.
As if the air itself had drawn you here,
And made the distance hesitate to appear.

No voice within it spoke of what might be—
Just how it moved... and brought you close to me.

The Awakening

I wandered through my days half-closed, half-bare,
A quiet world where nothing stirred my soul.
But then your presence moved within the air,
And every dim and silent place felt whole.

It wasn't thunder shaking me awake,
No sudden blaze or miracle undone—
Just how your fingers brushed my hand to make
A simple moment brighter than the sun.

You woke in me the joy I'd set aside,
A tenderness I thought I'd lost for good.
And standing there with you so close beside,
My heart remembered all it always could.

I opened then, the way a flower might—
Not to the world, but to your gentle light.

The Light Beyond the Veil

There was a veil between my heart and hope,
A fragile line I never crossed for long.
I lived within the limits I could hold,
And learned to carry what I felt was wrong.

No sudden light descended from above,
No sign was written in the dark of night—
Just how you stood, and something in your love
Made what I carried feel less tightly held.

You did not break the boundary I knew,
Nor call me from the place I learned to stay;
You simply stood—and something in me grew
Toward what I had not yet allowed to say.

The veil remained, but not the way it seemed—
It thinned enough to let your presence through.

The Beckoning Flame

A quiet warmth had settled in the dark,
Not distant light nor something set apart,
But something close—your presence like a spark
That moved through places I had closed in heart.

I felt it first in how you spoke my name,
A softness I had not prepared to hear.
No guiding star, no distant, holy flame—
Just how your voice made something draw me near.

It wasn't light that led me through the night,
But how your hand would find and steady mine.
And in that touch, the world grew less confined,
As if its edges shifted out of line.

I followed not a flame I could define—
Just how your warmth made something turn to mine.

A Song in the Dark

There was a time when night felt close and long,
When silence pressed too firmly to ignore.
It filled the spaces where I once felt strong,
And lingered where I'd spoken hope before.

Then came your voice—not louder than the dark,
Nor rising like a sound meant to command—
But something softer, leaving just a mark
Of warmth I had not planned to understand.

It wasn't music formed of distant things,
No choir carried through the open sky;
Just how your breath, in quiet utterings,
Made something in me answer back nearby.

Your voice did not remove what I had known—
It made the night feel less like mine alone.

Where Our Future First Appeared

I walked a road that did not quite reveal
What waited past the reach of what I knew.
Each step was taken more by habit still
Than any sense of where the path might move.

You did not point me toward some distant place,
Nor speak of what the days ahead might hold;
You simply stood, and in that quiet space
The air itself felt different than before.

Not that the world had opened wide at once,
Or something vast had formed before my sight—
But how the moment held a subtle sense
That more could come from standing in its light.

No future drawn, no promise to pursue—
Just how that moment felt... and included you.

The Calm I Found in You

The world grew heavy, pressing on my chest,
A quiet weight that lingered without end.
I carried it the way I carried breath,
Without expecting it to ever bend.

You did not promise anything would change,
Nor speak of ease or days without their strain;
You simply stayed, and in that quiet range
The weight I held felt different in its frame.

Your voice became a place where I could rest,
Not free from all the things I could not name—
But less alone in bearing what I kept,
And less confined within what once remained.

I did not lose the weight I carried through—
It simply felt less heavy next to you.

A Hand Extended

I lived in places shaped by quiet doubt,
Afraid to reach beyond what I could name.
I held to what I knew, and left without
Expecting anything to shift or change.

Then you were there—your hand not pulling mine,
Not urging me to rise before I could;
You simply stood, and let the moment find
A way to feel less guarded where I stood.

Your touch did not become a promise made,
But something steady I could choose to trust.
And in that space, the fear began to fade—
Not gone, but loosened slightly from its hold.

You took my hand, and nothing was replaced—
But something in me shifted... and made space

The Light in Your Hands

A distant glow once marked the edge of night,
A faint direction I could barely trace.
It lingered far beyond my steady sight,
And never quite arrived within my space.

Then you were near—no flame, no sudden sign,
No brilliance breaking through what I had known;
Just how your hand would rest in place with mine,
And make the moment feel less far, alone.

It wasn't light that showed me where to go,
Or something I could follow from afar—
But how your presence held a quiet glow
That did not ask me who or where you are.

I learned that light is not a thing we chase—
But something felt when we are held in place.

A Star to Follow

I used to look beyond what I could hold,
Toward distant things that promised something more.
The sky would stretch with answers left untold,
A quiet pull I could not quite ignore.

You did not shine from some unreachable height,
Nor draw me toward a path I could not see;
You simply stood, and in that steady light,
The world felt closer than it had to me.

No star had fallen, nothing split the sky,
No sign appeared to mark what this might prove—
Just how your presence did not pass me by,
And made the distance shift in how it moved.

I follow not what glimmers from above—
But what feels near... and answers me as love.

The Doorway of Desire

There was a doorway hidden in my life,
A place I'd learned to pass, but never stay.
I knew its shape, the outline of its frame,
Yet kept myself from turning fully in.

You did not move to force the hinges wide,
Nor press me toward what I was not prepared;
You simply stood, and in that quiet space,
The door felt less like something to be feared.

I breathed a little deeper than before,
And let the stillness settle where I stood.
Not drawn by want, nor pulled by sudden flame—
But by a sense that opening felt good.

The doorway stayed, not something overcome—
But something I could enter... step by step.

The Echo of Belief

There was a truth I kept just out of reach,
A quiet thought I chose not to pursue.
It lingered somewhere just beneath my speech,
But never formed in anything I knew.

You did not speak it plainly into place,
Nor shape it into something I could claim;
You simply looked—and in that steady gaze,
The silence held a slightly different frame.

It wasn't sudden, nothing fully clear,
No certainty I could at once receive—
Just how the quiet felt less bound by fear,
And made a little room for me to believe.

The truth remained, not something newly given—
But something in me heard... and leaned toward it.

A Glance Eternal

I saw you once, in nothing more than passing,
No grand design, no shift the world could claim.
The moment held, though time itself kept moving,
And yet it did not feel to me the same.

You didn't speak, and neither did I answer,
No promise formed between what we could see.
But something quiet moved beneath the surface,
A stillness settling somewhere deep in me.

It wasn't fate, nor anything so certain,
No voice declaring what our lives would be.
Just how your eyes met mine without resistance—
And left behind a sense of clarity.

Not love complete, nor something I could prove—
But something real... and asking me to move.

The Instant's Bloom

The moment came and lingered in the air,
As if the world had paused to let it be.
No sound announced it, nothing laid it bare—
Just something opening quietly in me.

Your presence felt like light before its rise,
A soft unfolding just beyond my sight.
I could not name the truth within your eyes,
But something in them leaned me toward the light.

No grand design revealed what this might mean,
No future drawn across a waiting sky;
Just how the space between us felt unseen,
Yet fuller than the reasons I could try.

A single glance, and still I cannot prove—
Why something small began to feel like truth.

The Light You Brought

Beneath the trees, where shifting shadows lay,
I caught your face within the moving light.
The afternoon seemed altered in its sway,
As though the day itself had drawn in sight.

The sunlight lingered longer than before,
It moved across your skin as if it knew
Some quiet thing I could not name or hold,
Yet felt more present simply standing near you.

Your laughter rose—no promise in its sound,
Yet something in it settled deep and clear.
Not peace declared, but something newly found,
A softening that made the moment near.

No flame pronounced, no fate to overprove—
Just how your light made room for something new.

A World of Two

The crowd moved on, a restless, shifting tide,
A thousand moments passing in a blur.
Yet something in me quieted inside
The instant I became aware of you.

Not that the world had vanished from its place,
Nor that the noise had suddenly grown still—
But how your presence gathered into space
And gently bent the air around my will.

You didn't call me from the moving scene,
Or draw me from the life I understood;
You simply stood—and something in between
Felt briefly held, and strangely, quietly good.

Not all the world reduced to only two—
But something there... that felt enough with you.

The Dawn of Us

The dawn had barely touched the edge of sky
When first I noticed light within your gaze.
Not something sudden I could justify,
But something shifting quietly in place.

It wasn't fire rising through my chest,
No sweeping truth that overtook my breath—
Just how the moment seemed to lean and rest
As if it held a meaning underneath.

No word could carry what I almost knew,
No language shape the space your presence made.
Yet something in me turned itself toward you,
As though a hidden path had been relayed.

The morning opened slowly into view—
And something in me opened toward you.

Where Your Love Began to Grow

My heart had settled into quiet ground,
A field that held but did not seem to rise.
It carried what was lost without a sound,
And kept its distance from imagined skies.

You did not come to fill it all at once,
Or press it toward a bloom it could not keep;
You stayed, and in that patience, something soft
Began to stir beneath what once was still.

No sudden change announced what might unfold,
No color forced its way into the gray—
Just how your presence lingered long enough
For something there to turn a different way.

Not yet in bloom, not something I could show—
But something in that ground... had started slow.

Love's Gentle Dawn

The dawn arrived without a need to prove
What light might mean or what the day might bring.
It moved across the land in quiet hues,
And let each thing become what it would be.

You did not promise mornings free from weight,
Nor speak of days untouched by what they hold;
You simply stood within the rising light,
And made the moment feel less sharply cold.

The world remained the same in form and shape,
Yet something in its presence shifted near.
Not brighter than before in any claim—
But softer, somehow easier to bear.

The dawn did not declare what love might do—
It simply rose... and found me next to you.

The Harbor of the Heart

I drifted through a stretch of open days,
Where nothing held me long enough to stay.
The waters moved without a steady shape,
And carried more than I could turn away.

You did not call me in from where I was,
Nor anchor me before I understood;
You simply stayed, and in that quietness,
The distance felt less constant than it could.

I did not find a harbor set in place,
No shore that ended all I wandered through—
But something in your presence held a space
That felt less open... standing next to you.

Not fully home, not something I could claim—
But less alone within what I became.

A Seed of Hope

A fragile hope had settled, faint and small,
So slight it barely stirred beneath my breath.
I carried it without much thought at all,
As something not yet strong enough to test.

You did not bring it suddenly to bloom,
Or force it into something it could show;
You stayed, and in that steady, quiet room,
It found a way to shift, and then to grow.

No burst of color marked what had begun,
No sign declared what might become of it—
Just how your presence lingered long enough
To let it rise, and slowly not resist.

What once was still has not yet fully grown—
But something in me no longer stands alone.

The Gift You Placed on Me

I carried weight I never thought to name,
A quiet burden settled into place.
It moved with me, and always felt the same,
A part of what I learned I had to face.

You did not take it from me as I stood,
Nor speak of ways it might be set aside;
You simply stayed, and in that understood
Something in me felt less inclined to hide.

No crown was placed, no title given form,
No sudden rise to something I could claim—
Just how your voice, in speaking me as known,
Made what I carried feel less tightly framed.

The weight remained, but not the way it grew—
It shifted... just by being seen by you.

The Thread
Between Our Hearts

There is a thread that runs from you to me,
So slight it nearly vanishes from view.
I cannot say just where its edges be,
Only that something draws me close to you.

It isn't formed by anything declared,
Nor placed by hands that shape what we might claim;
It moves beneath the things we've never shared,
A quiet pull that does not speak its name.

And when the world expands beyond our sight,
And distance bends the meaning of what's near,
It still remains—unseen, but held in light,
A subtle line I feel when you are here.

Not something proved, nor something I can start—
Just something felt... that lingers in the heart.

Waiting for Your Light

I used to look beyond what I could hold,
Toward distant signs that something might appear.
Each day returned the same as it had told,
And left me standing where the view was clear.

Then something changed—not outward, not defined,
But how the moment settled where you stood.
You did not shine from some far distant line—
You simply stayed, and something there felt good.

I am not watching for what may arrive,
Nor searching past the place where I remain;
I see your light in ways that feel alive,
Not breaking through, but softening the same.

I do not wait for something yet to be—
Your presence shifts what waiting means to me.

The Glass Wing

My heart had moved like something made too thin,
A fragile wing that feared the slightest air.
It held itself in carefulness within,
Unwilling still to risk what might be there.

You did not reach to mend what time had worn,
Nor force it back to what it could not be;
You simply touched the places left untorn,
And let them stay as they were, quietly.

And in that space, without a need to prove,
The fractures felt less fixed than they had seemed.
Not healed at once, nor suddenly removed—
But something in them shifted, softly freed.

The wing remains, not fully strong or whole—
But moves a little more... within your hold.

The Silent Bell

A quiet longing lingered in my chest,
A bell that never quite had found its sound.
It waited not for anything expressed—
Just held its silence, steady and unbound.

You did not strike it into sudden song,
Nor pull a note from where it could not give;
You simply stayed, and in that staying long,
It felt as though the stillness learned to live.

No echo broke across the evening air,
No sound declared what might begin or end—
Just something faint, a trembling almost-there,
That moved as though it might begin to bend.

The bell is still—not fully voiced or true—
But something in its silence leans toward you.

The Lighthouse Beam

I moved through spaces shaped by restless sound,
Where every turn felt wider than before.
The dark was not a thing that closed me in—
But something I had learned to carry more.

You did not rise as something set apart,
No towering light to separate the way;
You simply stood, and in that steady part,
The distance felt less certain than the day.

It wasn't guidance drawn from far ahead,
Nor something fixed to lead me safely through—
But how your presence held what I had held,
And made it feel less endless next to you.

I did not leave the night I wandered near—
It only felt... less distant with you here.

Where Longing Learned Your Name

Desire once moved restless through my days,
A quiet pull that never seemed to stay.
It had no place to settle or to rest,
Just something felt, then carried on its way.

You did not claim it or give it a form,
Nor draw it into something I could name;
You simply stood—and in that steady warmth,
The feeling shifted, though it stayed the same.

Not less in ache, but different in its tone,
A softening I could not quite explain.
As if what wandered once had found a place
Not fixed, but willing now to still remain.

Not fully known, nor something I could prove—
But something in me leaned... and leaned to you.

The Bridge You Helped Me Cross

There was a space I did not move beyond,
A distance shaped by what I could not trust.
I stood within it, knowing it was there,
But never sure it could be safely crossed.

You did not ask me to step further on,
Nor urge me past what I could not yet see;
You simply stood, and in that quiet span,
The space itself felt less like something fixed.

It did not close, nor vanish from its place,
Nor turn to something I could leave behind—
But how you stayed made crossing feel less far,
As if the distance shifted in my mind.

The space remains, but not the way it grew—
I move within it... differently with you.

The Star That Stayed With Me

I used to look for something set apart,
A distant sign to steady where I'd go.
The sky would stretch beyond what I could hold,
And offer more than I could come to know.

You did not shine from some unreachable height,
Nor call me toward a place I could not see;
You simply stayed, and in that steady light,
The world felt closer than it had to me.

No star had fallen, nothing split the sky,
No sign appeared to tell me what was true—
Just how your presence did not pass me by,
And made the distance shift... because of you.

I look no longer far for what I love—
But notice what remains... when you are near.

What Love Drew from the Deep

A quiet depth lay settled in my chest,
Its surface still, its movement rarely shown.
I knew it held more than I could express,
But left it there, as something left alone.

You did not reach to draw it into light,
Nor press it toward a form it could not keep;
You simply stayed, and in that patient nearness,
It found its way to rise from where it slept.

No sudden change declared what had begun,
No break in stillness marked what had been stirred—
Just how the surface shifted in the sun,
And held what once had gone unseen, unheard.

What surfaced did not ask to be defined—
Just something long within me... now aligned.

The Whisper That Became Your Name

A quiet whisper followed where I moved,
A presence I could feel but never trace.
It lingered just beneath what I could prove,
And moved with me from place to place to place.

It did not speak, nor form a shape I knew,
Just something near that would not disappear.
A sense that something waited out of view,
Without a voice to make its meaning clear.

Then you were there—not changing what it was,
Nor turning it to something fully known;
But how you stood allowed it to become
Less distant than it ever had been shown.

It does not speak, nor name what it might do—
But something in its quiet... sounds like you.

The Place
Your Voice Could Reach

I moved through spaces shaped by what I feared,
Where every sound returned to where it came.
The walls held more than what I thought I heard,
And gave it back without a different name.

You did not call me out from where I stood,
Nor break the silence I had come to know;
You simply spoke, and something in your voice
Made what I heard feel different as it moved.

It did not change the shape of where I was,
Nor lift me from the place I understood—
But how it reached allowed the space to hold
Something it never fully had before.

I stand where I have always stood in view—
But something there can hear... because of you.

The Place You Waited for Me

A single tree once stood along my way,
Its branches wide, its shadow calm and still.
I passed it often, never choosing to stay,
Just something there I never tried to feel.

You did not place it there, nor call it mine,
Nor name it something I was meant to see;
You simply stood within that quiet line,
And let the moment open gradually.

You did not move me faster than I could,
Nor pull me from the path I understood;
You stayed where light and shade could both remain,
And let me come as I had always came.

The place remains, not something I outgrew—
But something I can enter... when with you.

The Flame You Kept For Us

A quiet fire flickered out of sight,
Too faint to warm the cold I carried through.
It lived without a claim to shape or light,
Just something small that never fully grew.

You did not reach to force it into flame,
Nor feed it more than it was made to hold;
You simply stayed, and in that steady place,
It felt less hidden than it had before.

No sudden rise declared what it might be,
No blaze appeared to mark a turning point—
Just how the ember held more steadily,
As if it learned to live without the noise.

The fire remains, not something strong or proved—
But something still... and somehow less removed.

The Life We Paint Together

A canvas lingered somewhere in my days,
Unmarked, though not entirely left alone.
I saw its space, but never chose to stay
Long enough to call its surface home.

You did not fill it with a sudden form,
Nor press it toward a shape I had to see;
You simply stood, and in that quiet warmth,
The space itself felt less uncertain to me.

A color came—not placed, but slowly found,
A trace that held where once there had been none.
Not yet a picture I could name or sound—
Just something forming, line by careful line.

The canvas waits, not something fully known—
But something we are learning... as we go.

The Bond That Never Faltered

Between our hearts there moves a quiet thread,
Not fixed in place, nor held by what we say.
It shifts with all the things we leave unsaid,
And changes as the moments shape the day.

You did not bind it into something sure,
Nor hold it fast against what time might do;
You simply stayed, and made it feel more clear
That something there was steady... next to you.

It does not hold because it cannot break,
Nor stand untouched by all that life may send—
But something in it does not turn away,
Even when it learns again to bend.

Not something proven, fixed, or made to stay—
But something that remains... in how we stay.

III
The Deepening

◆

"To be known is not to be completed—
but to be met, again and again."

The Promise in Your Eyes

You never spoke a vow, yet something stayed
Within the way your gaze would meet my own.
Not something formed or suddenly conveyed—
But something I had felt, though not yet known.

You did not write it into air or night,
Nor place it where a promise could be named;
You simply looked—and in that steady sight,
The moment held more weight than what was claimed.

It wasn't certainty I could define,
Nor something fixed beyond what we could see—
Just how your eyes would return to mine,
And make that turning feel like honesty.

No vow declared, no truth I could construe—
But something in your seeing... stayed as true.

The Way Your Eyes Unfold

Your eyes would speak before you chose a word,
A quiet language I had come to read.
Not something loud, nor something I had heard—
But something shown in how you chose to be.

They did not promise more than they could hold,
Nor shape a future I could safely claim;
They simply stayed, and in that steady role,
They made the present feel less undefined.

I learned you not through anything you said,
But how your gaze would meet me where I stood—
Not asking more, nor leaving what we had,
But holding it in ways that felt like good.

Your eyes don't open all they might reveal—
But show enough... for something there to feel.

The Bond We Never Had to Name

Between us moved a closeness hard to place,
Not held by words, nor needing to be said.
It lived within the space we chose to face,
And grew in all the moments left unread.

We did not name it, shape it into form,
Nor press it into something we could claim;
It stayed beneath the shifting and the warm,
A quiet thread that did not ask for name.

It did not hold because it could not break,
Nor stand untouched by all that time might send—
But something in it did not turn away,
Even when it learned again to bend.

Not something fixed, nor something overgrown—
But something lived... and slowly, deeply known.

The Vow Made in Our Silence

No vow was spoken, yet something remained—
Not formed in words, nor carried into air.
It lived between what neither of us named,
But felt in how we chose to stay there.

You did not promise what you could not keep,
Nor shape devotion into something said;
You simply stood, and in that quiet deep,
The moment held more truth than what we pled.

It wasn't fixed, nor something we could prove,
Nor sealed beyond what time might rearrange—
Just how we stayed, and in that staying, moved
Toward something that was willing still to change.

No vow declared, no claim we had to prove—
But something formed... in how we chose to move.

Where Quiet Turns to Trust

It wasn't words that brought the trust to rise,
Nor something spoken into being true;
It formed within the space where silence lies,
And how that space was held between us two.

You did not ask for more than I could give,
Nor test the ground beneath what I could bear;
You simply stayed, and in that way of being,
The quiet felt less fragile than before.

It did not come as something fully known,
Nor settle into something I could claim—
But how we stood made something slowly grow,
A steadiness that did not need a name.

Trust did not speak, nor ask for us to prove—
It came to rest... in how we chose to move.

The Compass of the Soul

My heart no longer turns to distant signs,
Nor searches skies for where it might belong.
It moves instead within these present lines,
And learns to stay where it has been all along.

No unseen hand directs me where to go,
No star insists on what my path must prove;
But something in the way we come to know
Has taught this restless compass how to move.

It does not point to something yet to find,
Nor promise what the future might reveal—
It steadies in the nearness we have made,
And rests within the truth of what is real.

No longer drawn by what I could not see—
It holds its place... in what has come to be.

The Flame that Will Not Die

A quiet flame has settled where we stand,
Not rising loud, nor asking to be shown.
It lives within the things we understand,
And in the ways we've learned to stay our own.

It does not burn beyond what it can hold,
Nor promise more than we have come to know;
But moves in how we meet what we are told,
And keeps its warmth in all we choose to grow.

There are still nights where it feels less than clear,
Still winds that press against what we have made—
But something in it does not disappear,
Even when its light begins to fade.

Not fire untouched, nor something we deny—
But something lived... that does not need to die.

The Unseen Shore

We do not stand upon a distant shore,
Nor move toward something waiting far ahead.
We stand within what we have chosen for,
And learn to live inside what has been said.

There is no place where all the waves grow still,
No edge where longing finally disappears—
But something in the way we choose to feel
Has made the waters different through the years.

The storms still rise, the tides still shift their claim,
The distance comes in ways we cannot plan—
Yet something in us does not move the same,
Because we stay, and hold what we began.

No shore revealed, no final place to prove—
Just how we stand... and choose again to move.

The Bloom Beyond the Frost

There is no season where the frost is gone,
No final spring untouched by what has been.
The bloom we hold is something carried on
Within the cold, not waiting past it.

It does not rise because the storm has passed,
Nor wait for warmth to grant it room to grow;
It learns to live within the weight that lasts,
And finds its strength in what it comes to know.

There are still days where it feels pressed and small,
Still nights where it seems easier to close—
Yet something in it does not break at all,
Because it lives... within the life we chose.

Not something spared, nor something kept above—
But something growing... in the work of love.

The River Without End

The river does not run toward something new,
Nor seek a place where all its turns are done.
It moves within the course it travels through,
And shapes itself by how it has begun.

It does not rush to reach a final place,
Nor claim the end as something it must find;
It learns to hold its movement and its pace,
And stays within the shape it has defined.

There are still bends that neither of us know,
Still depths that shift beneath what we can see—
Yet something in the way we choose to flow
Has made the current less uncertainly.

No end to reach, no final truth to prove—
Just how we move... and choose again to move.

The First Breath

The first breath was not when we began,
Nor in the moment everything felt new;
It came much later, when we chose to stand
Within the weight of what we had come through.

No sudden light, no feeling we could claim,
No certainty that rose without its test—
Just how we stayed, returning just the same,
And learned to let the quiet do the rest.

It happened somewhere in the in-between,
Where words had thinned, and meaning had to stay;
Not what we felt, but what we chose to keep
When easier roads had turned themselves away.

The first breath came when leaving lost its place—
And we remained... and chose the same shared space.

Promises in Silence

No promise formed in words we could recall,
No vow pronounced to hold what we had made;
Yet something in the way we chose to stay
Felt stronger than what language could persuade.

It lived within the pauses we would keep,
The spaces where no answer had to come;
Not filled with fear, nor pressed for us to speak—
But held because we did not choose to run.

No future claimed, no certainty declared,
No path made clear beyond what we could see—
Just how we stood, and how we chose to bear
The weight of what we were... becoming to be.

Some promises are never said aloud—
But lived in how we stay... when staying's hard.

The Nearness We Did Not Name

There was a closeness neither of us named,
A nearness that did not require a word.
It moved between the things we never framed,
Yet shaped the way each silence could be heard.

It wasn't something spoken into form,
Nor something either of us tried to claim;
It grew in all the ways we kept it warm,
Without the need to ever call its name.

No distance broke what neither of us defined,
No measure held what neither tried to prove—
Just how we stayed, and in that staying found
A way to let the nearness slowly move.

Not something named, nor something to defend—
But something lived... again, and then again.

The Weight We Learned to Hold

There came a weight we could not set aside,
Not something love would lift or make undone.
It stayed with us, and moved from side to side,
A truth we carried... rather than outrun.

You did not ask me to be less than real,
Nor hide the parts that made the burden grow;
You simply stayed, and in that staying still,
The weight became less lonely in its hold.

It did not break, nor fade, nor disappear,
But something in it shifted as we stood—
Not lighter, no—but somehow easier
To bear within the shape of something good.

Love did not free us from what we must hold—
It made us strong enough... to hold it both.

The Quiet Between Us

There was a quiet neither of us feared,
Not empty, not a space we had to fill.
It lived between the things we once had said,
And lingered there... because we chose it still.

No need to speak what both of us could feel,
No rush to name what neither had to prove;
The quiet held what words could not reveal,
And shaped the way we learned to stay and move.

It wasn't absence, nor a lack of sound—
But something full that did not need a voice.
A place where what we were could still be found,
Because we stayed... and chose what we had chose.

Not silence lost, nor something left behind—
But quiet kept... because we both remained.

What Stayed Without Words

There were no words to hold what we became,
No language shaped to carry what we knew.
Yet something in the quiet stayed the same,
And did not fade when silence settled through.

We did not speak to prove what still remained,
Nor reach for sound to steady what we felt;
It lived within the space we both sustained,
A truth that did not ask itself to be held.

No vow was formed, no promise set in place,
No claim declared to guard what we had grown—
Just how we stayed, and in that steady space,
What mattered most was never left alone.

Some things endure beyond what words can prove—
What stayed with us... was never said, but moved.

The Space We Chose to Keep

There was a space we neither tried to close,
Nor filled with all the things we could have said.
It stayed between us, open as it was,
A quiet place where something deeper led.

We could have named it, shaped it into form,
Or pressed it into something we could claim;
But something in us chose to leave it warm,
And let it live without a given name.

It did not distance what we held as near,
Nor break the thread that moved between our hands—
It gave us room to meet what we might fear,
Without demanding we must understand.

Not every space is meant to disappear—
Some spaces stay... because we keep them clear.

The Way We Came Back

There were still moments when we turned away,
When distance formed in ways we did not plan.
Not out of loss, nor something we would say—
But simply part of being who we are.

We did not hold each other past what's real,
Nor force return before it could be true;
But something in the way we chose to feel
Would lead us back, again, and back to you.

No perfect path, no promise without strain,
No love untouched by all that life will send—
Just how we learned to come back through the same,
And meet again without pretending end.

Not that we never wandered from the place—
But that we found... our way back to that space.

What Did Not Turn Away

There were still things that asked us both to bend,
To face what neither of us thought we would.
Moments that tested where we chose to stand,
And what we held as something truly good.

We could have turned, and let the distance grow,
Or left the weight for one alone to bear;
But something in us did not choose to go—
It stayed, and met what waited for us there.

No strength declared, no triumph set in light,
No victory shaped for others to admire—
Just how we did not leave when it grew tight,
And held what stayed within the pressing fire.

Not that the weight was less, or easier to see—
But something stayed... and did not cease to be.

The Shape of Trust

Trust did not come as something we could name,
Nor settle in a moment fully known.
It formed within the ways we stayed the same,
Even as all the rest had changed its tone.

It was not built from promises alone,
Nor kept by words we offered in their place;
It lived in how we chose to stand and own
The truth of what we carried face to face.

There were still questions neither of us solved,
Still edges we had yet to understand—
Yet something in the way we stayed involved
Gave trust a shape no doubt could quite unhand.

Not fixed, nor flawless, certain, or above—
But something formed... in how we chose to love.

IV
The Breaking

""Not everything breaks at once—
some things change until they are gone."

Where Your Touch Still Lingers

Your touch remains in places I can't reach—
Not where you were, but where I still recall.
It comes unasked, without a way to leave,
A quiet presence moving through it all.

I try to name it something I can place,
A memory I might one day release—
But it returns in moments without shape,
And settles where I thought I'd finally have peace.

You are not here, and still I feel the trace,
Not strong, not whole—just something that remains.
Not ghost, not dream, not anything I face—
But something living underneath the pain.

Some things don't leave, no matter what we do—
Your touch is one... I carry without you.

The Rose That Couldn't Last

The rose you gave has folded into time,
Its edges dry, its color almost gone.
I keep it still, though it no longer lives,
As if it knows what I am holding on.

It once was soft enough to mark the air,
A quiet thing that did not need to prove—
But now it breaks beneath the slightest touch,
The way we do when we have something to lose.

I do not keep it for what it once was,
Nor for the way it made the moment feel—
I keep it because letting go of it
Would mean accepting something far too real.

Some things we hold because we cannot say—
If they are gone... or we just stayed too long.

The Rooms
Your Silence Filled

The rooms are not the same, though nothing's changed.
The walls still stand, the windows still let light.
But something in the air has rearranged,
And made the space feel wider than it should.

Your voice is gone—but not in any way
That leaves the silence clean or easy still.
It lingers, not as sound, but as a weight
That moves from room to room against my will.

I walk through places we once passed without
A thought of how they held what we had made—
And now each corner seems to carry more
Than I can name, and more than I can face.

The house is not empty—
It just no longer knows what to do with me.

The Vanished Star

You were not meant to vanish like a light
That leaves the sky without a trace behind.
There should have been some warning in the dark,
Some sign the night was learning to unwind.

But you were there—and then you simply weren't.
No shift I saw, no moment I could name.
Just how the sky kept holding where you burned,
As if it did not know you had changed.

I still look up, though nothing answers back,
Though reason tells me what I already know.
There are some habits grief does not release—
Some ways the heart refuses not to go.

The sky remains—
but not the way it did when you were in it.

The Tide that Took too Much

The tide went out and did not give it back.
That's how it feels, no matter what they say.
They speak of cycles, how the waves return—
But not of what is taken when they go.

I stood there thinking I could still recover
Some piece of what had slipped beneath the pull.
But there are losses that don't scatter clean—
They take the whole of what they came to hold.

The water moves like nothing has been changed,
As if it did not carry part of me.
And maybe that's the hardest thing to face—
The world goes on... without accounting me.

The tide returns—
but never what it took.

The Echo of Your Name

Your name still comes to me without consent,
In quiet moments I don't try to fill.
Not loud, not clear—just present in a way
That makes the silence harder to sit with.

I do not say it—but it finds its shape
In how I think, in how I almost speak.
It moves beneath the things I try to hold,
A sound that never settles into sleep.

I thought that time would soften what remains,
Or make it easier to let it pass—
But some things don't grow quiet when they fade,
They just become... the background of the past.

Your name is not a word I choose to say—
It's something that still speaks... when I don't.

The Picture I Still Hold

Your picture hangs where it has always been.
I have not moved it, though I could have done.
It stays because I don't know what would change
If I admitted you are truly gone.

I touch the glass the way I used to reach
For something I believed would still respond.
But nothing answers—nothing ever does—
And still I come back here and do it again.

They say that holding on will slow the grief,
That letting go is something I must learn.
But no one tells you how to put down
A life that never asked you not to stay.

The picture stays—
because I don't know how to move it... without moving you.

The River Grief Carved Deep

There is a place where something gave way in me—
Not all at once, but slowly, over time.
What used to hold has shifted out of reach,
And left a depth I do not try to name.

It moves beneath the things I try to do,
A current I can feel but cannot see.
Not always strong—but never fully gone,
It waits in quiet places underneath.

Sometimes I catch a glimpse of what was there,
Not clearly—just enough to recognize.
And then it's gone again, without a trace,
As if it knows I'm not prepared to stay.

I do not follow where it seems to lead—
I just... live over what it's made of me.

The Clock That Outlasted Us

The clock keeps time as if nothing has changed.
It does not slow, or hesitate, or ask.
It moves the same as it did when you were here,
And that is what I cannot reconcile.

I watch it sometimes longer than I should,
As if it might explain what I can't hold.
But it just moves—indifferent to the fact
That something ended it cannot record.

There was a rhythm once I understood.
Something we kept without needing to try.
Now time continues—but without that shape,
And I don't know what I am moving through.

The clock goes on—
but I no longer know what it is measuring.

The Garden of Regret

There are things I would undo if I could,
Not all of it—just moments held too tight.
What once felt small, misunderstood as good,
Returns with weight I did not see that night.

They come uncalled, in ways I can't prepare,
Not as clear scenes, but questions left behind—
The kind that linger in the open air,
Without a place where answers come to mind.

I do not seek them out, yet still they stay,
Revisiting the things I chose not to see.
And each return reveals a different way
The past still shifts what I have come to be.

I do not know if this is grief, or truth—
Or what remains when there is no more "you."

That Haunts Me Still

There are brief hours when I do not feel
The weight of what no longer can be found.
The day moves on, almost enough to seem
Untouched by all that is no longer around.

Then something small—a shift I cannot name—
Returns it all without a warning sign.
Not your hand, no—but something just the same,
An absence I still register as mine.

I do not reach the way I used to do,
Yet still it comes, unbidden, incomplete.
A trace of what I once believed was you,
Now living where my body feels defeat.

I cannot tell if time will make it fade—
Or teach me how to live with what has stayed.

The Rose You Left Behind

The rose remains where I have left it still,
Untouched, though I have thought to move it on.
Not out of care—but something in my will
Refuses proof that what we had is gone.

Its color fades in ways I didn't see
Until the change had settled into place.
It holds less form than what it used to be,
Yet still it keeps a kind of quiet trace.

I do not look at it with constant need,
But when I do, it speaks without a voice—
How something living can become a thing
We keep, not out of love, but lack of choice.

I leave it where it is, though I could move—
Not sure what changes... if I let it lose.

The House We Left Behind

I do not go there often, though I could,
The door still stands the way it always has.
From where I stand, it looks the way it should—
No sign of what has altered in its past.

But stepping in, the air does not agree.
Not empty—no—but something out of place.
A shift I feel that does not let me be
The person who once moved through every space.

I thought I'd hold each memory intact,
That nothing there would slip beyond my view.
But even now, some details fade to black,
And I don't know what that is asking me to do.

I cannot tell if leaving helps me heal—
Or if returning keeps what once was real.

The Star that Once Was Yours

I do not look the way I used to look
Toward skies that once held something I believed.
Nothing has changed—and yet something is took
From how I see what once I had received.

There was a time I trusted things would stay,
Not endlessly—but long enough to hold.
A quiet sense they would not slip away,
Or turn to something distant, dim, and cold.

I do not think like that as I did then.
The sky remains, but not in how I see.
Still, there are moments I forget again,
And look as if something might return to me.

But what I know returns before it's through—
The sky is still... just not the one I knew.

What the Tide Returned to Me

The tide once left me empty on the shore,
Its absence taking more than I could name.
I stood with less than what I had before,
And nothing in the water spoke the same.

They say the sea returns what it receives,
That time will bring a balance to the loss.
But what came back was not what memory grieves,
Nor anything that answered to its cost.

It brought no trace of what had slipped away,
No voice, no warmth, no echo I could claim—
Just something altered in the light of day,
A different weight that did not feel the same.

The tide returns—but not what once was me—
It leaves me with what I must learn to be.

The Silent Song

The song you sang does not return the same,
It comes in fragments I cannot complete.
A note, a breath, a shadow of its name—
Then silence falls again before it meets.

I try to follow where it used to lead,
But lose it somewhere I cannot retrace.
It isn't gone—but not enough to keep,
A sound that will not fully take its place.

It lingers just beneath what I can hear,
Not loud enough to comfort or restore—
But present in a way that draws it near,

Then leaves me with its absence even more.
The song remains—but never as it was—
A thing I hear... and lose, because it does.

The Gate We Couldn't Keep

The gate still stands, though no one passes through,
Its hinges slow, its frame no longer sure.
It opens not the way it used to do,
Nor holds the shape it once could still endure.

I touch it as if something might return,
As if the past still answers when I try.
But time has changed what it refused to learn—
Some things give way, no matter how we try.

We built it with what we believed would last,
A place where nothing fragile could divide.
But something in us shifted as we passed,
And left it open on a different side.

The gate remains—but not for what we keep—
Just something there... that neither of us keeps.

The Vine That Couldn't Hold

The vine once climbed where both our hands had placed
Its tender reach along a borrowed wall.
It stretched toward light, and in that fragile space,
We thought its growth might outlast all.

I gave it more than what the season gave,
And watched for signs that it would still remain.
But some things fade in ways we cannot save,
No matter how we tend them through the strain.

The leaves fell slowly, one by one, unseen,
Not all at once—but never quite restored.
And in that loss, I saw what it had been,
Not what I hoped it still might move toward.

The vine let go—not something I could hold—
It stayed as long... as it was meant to grow.

The Dream
That Wouldn't Leave

I wake, and still you linger in the room,
Not fully there—but not entirely gone.
A trace that does not vanish with the light,
But shifts its shape as morning carries on.

I know the truth—I've said it to myself,
In words that should have settled what is real.
But something in me does not follow through,
And keeps what I have learned I should not feel.

You move in ways that memory allows,
Not as you were—but something I recall.
And even knowing what the truth is now,
I still respond as if you hear the call.

Some dreams remain beyond what waking proves—
Not because they stay... but because something does.

The Glass We Couldn't Mend

The glass once held what we believed was clear,
A surface bright enough to trust the view.
But something in it fractured over time,
And changed the way the light would pass it through.
I tried to place each piece where it had been,

To hold the shape that once had made it whole.
But cracks don't ask for meaning when they spread—
They move until they take what they can hold.

We saw it break before it fully did,
Yet stayed as if the end could be delayed.
But some things fail in ways we cannot fix,
No matter how we wish they might have stayed.

The glass remains—but never as before—
It holds the light... but not what it was for.

V

The Faithful

<hr>

"What remains is not what we expected—
but it is still ours to carry."

The Hours Without You

The hours pass, though not the way they did,
They move, but something in them has been changed.
I mark their rhythm, though I no longer live
Inside the shape where you and I were named.

Your absence does not leave the moments clean,
It settles in the spaces I still keep.
Not loud, not sharp—but something in between,
A quiet weight that does not fully sleep.

I do not count them as I once had done,
Nor measure what they bring me closer to.
They simply move, and I remain within
A life that learned to hold without its "you."

The hours remain—not something to undo—
But something I now live... because I do.

The Fading Flame

The flame we held no longer burns the same,
Its light reduced, its reach no longer wide.
It does not rise to answer to its name,
Nor hold the warmth it once could not deny.

I do not chase what it has ceased to be,
Nor try to force its glow to reappear.
Some fires diminish without remedy,
And leave behind what will not disappear.

It is not gone—but changed beyond return,
A quieter thing than what it once had shown.
And in that shift, I've had to slowly learn
To let it be... without needing it whole.

The flame remains—but not for what it gave—
Just something I acknowledge... and still name.

The Chair That Waits
For You

The chair remains where it has always been,
Unmoved, unchanged, though everything has shifted.
It holds no claim on what we once lived in—
Just stands where something once had gently rested.

I do not sit and wait the way I did,
Nor look toward doors that no longer open.
But still it holds a trace of what once lived,
Not asking me to name it, or to hold it.

There was a time I thought it meant return,
That something left might find its way back through.
But now I see it simply lets me learn
How something stays... without becoming you.

The chair remains—not waiting as before—
Just something there... that does not ask for more.

The Silent Goodbye

You did not speak the words that marked the end,
No closing line to tell me where we stood.
It came instead in ways I could not name,
A shift I felt, but never understood.

I searched for something I could recognize,
A moment I could point to and define—
But endings don't announce themselves that way,
They settle in... and change the shape of time.

And now I live within what that became,
Not asking for the words I never heard.
The silence holds more truth than what we'd claim,
And leaves me with what cannot be deferred.

No final sound—but still it came to be—
A part of what remains... inside of me.

The Letter I Still Hold

The letter rests where I have kept it still,
Its ink now faint, its edges worn with time.
I do not read it as I once would feel,
But as a trace of something that was mine.

The words remain, though not the way they did,
They carry less of what I used to hear.
Not empty—no—but something changed within
The way they meet me now that you're not here.

I do not hold it as a thing to keep
What cannot be returned to what it was.
But something in it lets me still receive
The truth of what we were... because it was.

The letter stays—not asking me to choose—
Just something I can hold... and not refuse.

The Spark of Us

It wasn't what I thought it was back then—
Not something clear, or meant to always stay.
I named it more than what it could have been,
Because I did not know another way.

There was a spark, yes—but not what I knew,
Not something bound to everything I'd claim.
It lived within a moment passing through,
And I mistook its light for something named.

Now looking back, I see it differently—
Not less, not lost, not something I deny.
But just a start of what would come to be,
A truth I only learned by asking why.

The spark remains—but not as I once knew—
It was not all... but it was something true.

Unspoken Vows

There were no vows the way I used to say,
No promises that time could not undo.
We felt something—and I gave it that name,
Because I thought that feeling must be true.

We stood inside a moment without form,
And I believed it held what we would be.
But now I know that love does not perform
Its truth in things we think we instantly see.

The vow was not in what we thought we knew,
Nor in the silence I once called complete—
It came much later, in what we went through,
In how we chose to stay... or to retreat.

Not what we felt—but what we came to do—
That is the vow... that ever made it true.

A Moment's Truth

That moment was not everything I claimed,
Though I believed it held what we would be.
I gave it weight, and shaped it into name,
And called it truth before it could agree.

There was a truth—but not the one I knew,
Not something fixed inside a single place.
It changed with everything we later grew,
And what we learned to carry... or erase.

I do not look at it with loss or shame,
Nor try to make it less than what it gave—
But I no longer need to call it all,
Or make it something time was meant to save.

It was a moment—and it still is true—
But not the truth... I thought I always knew.

Timeless Connection

did not live outside of time and change,
Though once I thought it moved beyond it all.
I see it now within a different frame—
Something that rose... and something that could fall.

There was a bond, but not untouched by strain,
Not something time would leave entirely whole.
It moved through everything we could not name,
And changed the shape of how we came to hold.

I do not need to make it something fixed,
Or place it where it cannot shift again.
It lived, it changed, it gave, it also took—
And still remains... in ways I understand.

Not timeless as I once had tried to prove—
But something real... that taught me how to love.

The Beginning of Us

The beginning is not where I return,
Not something I can hold as it once was.
It lives within the things I came to learn,
And not within the way I named it first.

I thought it started everything I'd be,
That single moment shaping all ahead.
But now I see it differently—
A place we entered, not a place we stayed.

It gave us something neither could ignore,
A turning neither one of us could name.
But what it meant became so much more
In all we lost, and all that later came.

The start remains—but not as I once knew—
It lives now... in what we lived through.

The Endless Flame

The flame still lives, though not as it once burned,
It does not rise to answer what I knew.
Its heat has changed, its edges less defined,
A quieter thing than what it once could do.

It does not stand against all time and loss,
Nor claim a strength untouched by what has been.
It lives within the cost we did not stop,
And in the places we did not give in.

There were things it could not hold together,
And things it could not keep from falling through.
But something in it did not disappear—
It stayed... though not the way I wanted to.

The flame remains—not endless, not the same—
But something I still recognize as flame.

Across the Stars

There is no distance left for us to cross,
No space between that time has not revealed.
What once I thought could never suffer loss
Has shown me what it can, and cannot, hold.

I do not feel you moving through the night,
Nor sense you waiting somewhere I must go.
But something of you lives within my sight,
In ways I do not always need to know.

The distance now is not of space or sky,
But what remains between what was and is.
And still, I carry something I don't deny—
Not where you are... but what you were in this.

No stars to cross, no place to meet anew—
Just something here... that still remembers you.

Eternal Thread

There is a thread—but not as I once said,
Not something fixed beyond what time can move.
It did not bind us where I thought it led,
Nor hold us in the way I tried to prove.

It stretched, it strained, it nearly came undone,
It changed with every truth we could not keep.
And still—there's something I cannot outrun,
A line that runs beneath what lies asleep.

Not fate, not vow, not something made to last—
But something lived, and therefore still remains.
Not whole, not pure, not untouched by the past—
But present in the shape that memory names.

The thread is not what I once thought it knew—
It lives now... differently... but still runs through.

Love's Timeless Song

The song is not untouched by what has passed,
It does not rise the way it once began.
Its notes are shaped by everything that changed,
And all the things that did not go as planned.

It does not carry only what was good,
Nor sing as if the pain was not a part.
It holds the truth of everything it knew,
And moves within the chambers of the heart.

There are some notes that no longer return,
And others that have taken on new sound.
But something in it still allows me to hear
What once was lost... and still is somehow found.

The song remains—but not as it once moved—
It lives now... altered... but it still is true.

Beyond the Veil

There was a time I thought that love would stand
Beyond the reach of anything that ends—
Untouched by time, unshaken where it lands,
A truth no loss could ever make it bend.

I do not think that way as once I did.
I've seen what time can take, and what it leaves.
Not everything we held was meant to stay,
And not all love survives the way it's believed.

And still—there's something I cannot dismiss,
Not what we were, nor what we failed to keep—
But how it lives in ways I can't resist,
A presence moving quietly and deep.

Not past the veil—but here, within what grew—
I do not have you... but I carry you.

What We Chose to Keep

Not everything was meant to carry through,
Not every part could live beyond the strain.
There were things lost we could not make untrue,
And things we held that did not still remain.

But something stayed—not all, and not the same,
Not what we thought would always be preserved.
It wasn't built from promise, vow, or claim,
But something quieter... and more deserved.

We kept what did not ask to be restored,
Not what we wished, but what refused to leave.
A truth not shaped by what we once adored—
But what endured... because we still believed.

Not all was saved—but this, at least, was true:
What stayed with me... was something shaped by you.

The Shape of Staying

Staying was never what I thought it meant—
Not standing still, nor holding what we had.
It came in ways I could not represent,
In things that changed, and things that turned out bad.

It asked for more than I had known to give,
Not once—but over time, again, again.
Not just to love—but to remain and live
Inside what could not be undone by then.

It wasn't clean, or easy to define,
Not something formed in one decisive act.
It took its shape in all the in-between,
In how we faced what would not turn us back.

Staying is not what never moves away—
It's what remains... though everything has changed.

Love After Knowing

I did not know what love would ask of me
When first I named it something pure and whole.
I hadn't seen what I would come to see,
Or how it would reshape what I could hold.

It was not less—but never what I thought,
Not something fixed beyond what life would prove.
It carried more than what I thought it brought,
And changed the way I understood its truth.

I know it now—not fully, not complete—
But more than what I once believed was real.
Not just in what is given or received,
But what remains... when nothing else can heal.

Love after knowing is not what it seems—
It is what stays... when stripped of what we dreamed.

What Remains of Us

We are not what we were—and that is clear.
Not something time could hold in its first frame.
Too much has passed, too much has altered here,
For us to stand and call it still the same.

And yet—there's something I cannot deny,
Not in the past, nor something I pursue.
But in the way your presence does not die
Inside the life I've had to carry through.

Not all of us—but something still remains,
Not whole, not fixed, not untouched by what's gone.
But present in the shape that memory names,
And in the ways I still keep moving on.

We are not what we were—but something stays:
A trace of us... that time cannot erase.

The Glance Remembered

I thought that glance had given everything,
A moment holding all that we would be.
I named it truth, a kind of endless thing,
A beginning shaped by certainty.

But now I see it differently than then—
Not less, not lost, not something I outgrew—
But just the first of many ways we learned
What love could hold... and what it could not do.

It did not promise all that I believed,
Nor fail because it could not make it last.
It was a moment I have since received
As something changed by everything that passed.

That glance remains—not what I thought I knew—
But where it started... still feels somehow true.

---

*"What remains is not what we expected—
but it is still ours to carry."*

The Poet's Reflection

These poems were not written to preserve a moment—
but to understand what becomes of it.

A glance can feel like everything.
It can carry certainty, wonder,
the quiet belief that something has begun
that cannot be undone.

But life does not leave that moment untouched.

Love grows.
It changes.
It deepens in ways we don't expect—
and sometimes, it breaks in ways we cannot prevent.

This collection is not about love that remained perfect.
It is about love that was lived.

About what we held.
What we lost.
What we misunderstood.
And what, somehow, remained.

If you have ever looked back
on a moment that once meant everything—
and found that it still means something,
even after everything has changed—

then you understand this book.

You may not find the beginning again.

But you may find
that it never fully left you.

— John David Smith

The Blessing

May these poems meet you
not where you first believed in love,
but where you now understand it.

May they sit with what you've carried—
the moments you revisit,
the ones you question,
the ones that never quite left.

May you find peace
not in what could have stayed,
but in what still remains.
And if love has changed you—
even in ways you did not choose—

may you come to see
that something of it
was never wasted.

— John David Smith

Some beginnings do not end—
they become something else we learn to carry.

Reflection Guide

*For Personal Reflection, Couples, Book Clubs,
and Quiet Conversations*

Entering the Journey

Before beginning—or after finishing—take a moment to sit with this question:

What has love been for you?

Not what you hoped it would be...
but what it has actually become.

I. The Glance — Recognition

- Have you ever experienced a moment that felt like everything began at once? What did it mean to you then?

- Looking back, do you still understand that moment the same way? Why or why not?

- What did you believe love *was* at the beginning?

II. The Staying — Presence

- What does it mean to stay—when love is no longer new?

- Have you experienced a relationship where presence mattered more than passion?

- In your life, what has required you to remain when leaving would have been easier?

III. The Deepening — Knowing

- When did love shift from feeling... to understanding?

- What have you learned about another person that changed how you loved them?

- What does trust look like in your relationships—not in words, but in action?

IV. The Breaking — Loss

- What has love cost you?

- Have you ever had to carry the absence of someone who once felt essential?

- What remains in you from a relationship that no longer exists?

Take your time here. Some answers don't come quickly—and some don't come at all.

V. The Faithful — What Remains

- What have you chosen to keep, even after everything changed?

- How has your understanding of love matured over time?

- Can something still be meaningful... even if it did not last?

Closing Reflection (Sit with this gently)

What do you carry now...

that you didn't understand at the beginning?

For Couples (Optional Conversation Prompts)

- What part of our relationship has required the most growth from you?

- When have you felt most seen… without needing to explain yourself?

- What have we had to learn the hard way—and what has that taught us?

- What are we choosing to keep, even as we continue to change?

A Final Invitation

You don't have to answer every question.
You don't have to have clarity.

Just be honest with what comes.

Love is not always understood in the moment—
but it reveals itself in reflection.

Let this be a space

where you can listen
to what your own life is trying to say.

For a printable version of this reflection guide,
along with additional prompts and companion resources,
scan the QR code or visit:
www.scribeandcanvas.com/resources

Designed for personal reflection,
couples, book clubs,
and spaces where honest conversations are welcomed.

www.ingramcontent.com/pod-product-compliance
Lightning Source LLC
Chambersburg PA
CBHW050031110726
47973CB00033B/285/J